Good Housekeeping Cookery Club

*P*ASTA

Lyn Rutherford

EBURY PRESS
LONDON

First published 1994

1 3 5 7 9 10 8 6 4 2

Text and Photography © Ebury Press 1994

All rights reserved. No part of this publication may be reproduced, stored in a retrieval system, or transmitted in any form or by any means, electronic, mechanical, photocopying, recording or otherwise, without the prior permission of the copyright owners.

The expression GOOD HOUSEKEEPING as used in the title of the book is the trade mark of the National Magazine Company Limited and The Hearst Corporation, registered in the United Kingdom and USA, and other principal countries of the world, and is the absolute property of the National Magazine Company Limited and The Hearst Corporation. The use of this trade mark other than with the express permission of The National Magazine Company Limited or The Hearst Corporation is strictly prohibited.

First published in the United Kingdom in 1994 by
Ebury Press Random House, 20 Vauxhall Bridge Road, London SW1V 2SA

Random House Australia (Pty) Limited
20 Alfred Street, Milsons Point, Sydney,
New South Wales 2061, Australia

Random House New Zealand Limited
18 Poland Road, Glenfield,
Auckland 10, New Zealand

Random House South Africa (Pty) Limited
PO Box 337, Bergvlei, South Africa

Random House UK Limited Reg. No. 954009

A CIP catalogue record for this book is available from the British Library.

Managing Editor: JANET ILLSLEY
Design: SARA KIDD
Special Photography: KEN FIELD
Food Stylist: LYN RUTHERFORD
Photographic Stylist: SUZI GITTINGS
Techniques Photography: KARL ADAMSON
Food Techniques Stylist: ANNIE NICHOLS
Recipe Testing: EMMA-LEE GOW

The author would like to thank Deborah Greatrex and Margaret Brooker for their help with this book.

ISBN 0 09 178570 7

Typeset in Gill Sans by Textype Typesetters, Cambridge
Colour Separations by Magnacraft, London
Printed and bound in Italy by New Interlitho Italia S.p.a., Milan

CONTENTS

COOKERY NOTES

- Both metric and imperial measures are given for the recipes. Follow either metric or imperial throughout as they are not interchangeable.
- All spoon measures are level unless otherwise stated. Sets of measuring spoons are available in both metric and imperial sizes for accurate measurement of small quantities.
- Ovens should be preheated to the specified temperature. Grills should also be preheated. The cooking times given in the recipes assume that this has been done.

- If a stage is specified under freezing instructions, the dish should be frozen at the end of that stage.
- Size 2 eggs should be used except where otherwise specified.
- Use freshly ground black pepper unless otherwise specified.
- Use fresh rather than dried herbs unless dried herbs are suggested in the recipe.
- Always use freshly grated or shredded Parmesan, not ready-grated cheese.

INTRODUCTION

Pasta is one of the world's best loved foods. In Italy hardly a meal is served without it, and elsewhere in the world almost everyone has a favourite pasta dish. Hopefully this collection will inspire you to experiment and enjoy new pasta combinations.

All of the recipes will serve four generously as a main course; if accompanied by a salad and perhaps some good, crusty bread they will serve up to six. The only exceptions are the quick and simple recipes in the final chapter which are more suitable for a light lunch or informal supper, than a main course. As a starter, most of the recipes in this book will serve six or possibly eight, depending on appetites and the main course to follow.

With the exception of the filled pasta dishes, dried pasta can be used for all of the recipes. Indeed, unless you are going to prepare your own pasta I would recommend dried pasta over commercially produced 'fresh' types, which can be starchy and rather heavy.

Handmade pasta which has been carefully prepared from flour and fresh eggs, then rolled and stretched until paper-thin needs little cooking and is surprisingly light – almost melting in the mouth. If you have never tried making your own pasta, do give it a try. It is really as simple as pastry making and the equipment required is basically the same. Essentials are a rolling pin, metal pastry cutters, a sharp knife and, ideally, a pastry wheel. This is all you need to roll out and cut the dough. If making fresh pasta becomes a regular event, consider investing in a pasta machine which gives good uniform results and saves time and effort.

You will find that some pasta shapes are more suited to particular recipes than others. Large shapes and wide ribbons, for example, tend to work best in dishes where the other ingredients are on the chunky side. Smoother textured sauces are generally served with finer pastas, such as spaghetti or tagliarini. In a recipe where there is plenty of liquid I usually suggest tubes or shells to hold the sauce.

In other respects, the choice of pasta in a recipe is a personal one. I prefer egg pasta to green, for example, and have certain favourite shapes I like to eat. But if wholemeal pasta is your passion, or tomato is more to your taste, then by all means use your favourites. There are few hard and fast rules in cooking and pasta in particular lends itself beautifully to experimentation.

Finally, do take care to avoid overcooking pasta. Fresh pasta needs only the briefest cooking – so watch it carefully. For dried pasta I suggest you refer to the packet instructions, but use these as a guide only. The only way to ensure that fresh or dried pasta is properly cooked is to taste it. Before the end of the recommended cooking time, take a piece of pasta from the cooking pot and bite it – it should be cooked through but 'al dente' or firm to the bite.

DRIED PASTA SHAPES

1 Fusilli; 2 Long Fusilli; 3 Plain, Tomato and Spinach Fusilli; 4 Conchiglioni (large shells); 5 Capellini; 6 Plain and Spinach Tagliatelle; 7 Wholewheat Spaghetti; 8 Fettucine; 9 Lasagne (wavy-edged); 10 Plain and Spinach Lasagne; 11 Pappardelle; 12 Pastina; 13 Conchiglie (shells); 14 Cavatappi (corkscrews); 15 Penne (tubes).

HOMEMADE PASTA

Pasta is fun to prepare and you will find that the flavour of freshly cooked homemade pasta is incomparable. Best results are achieved if you use a special pasta flour, such as the fine-textured wheat flour 'type 00' which is available from Italian delicatessens and some large supermarkets. If unobtainable, the nearest equivalent is strong plain bread flour. The proportions are 100 g (3½ oz) flour to 1 egg (size 3).

QUANTITIES TO SERVE 4

PASTA RIBBONS
300 g (10 oz) '00' pasta flour
pinch of salt
3 eggs (size 3)
PASTA SHEETS
(for lasagne, ravioli etc)
200 g (7 oz) '00' pasta flour
pinch of salt
2 eggs (size 3)

335 CALS 100 G (3½ OZ)

1. Sift the flour and salt into a mound on a wooden board or clean work surface and make a well in the centre. Break the eggs into the well.

2. Using a fork, gently beat the eggs together, then gradually draw in the flour. Work from the inside of the flour well so the egg is not allowed to escape.

3. When the mixture begins to thicken, use your hands to mix to a firm but moist dough.

4. Clean the work surface free of crusty flour which could spoil the texture of the pasta, then knead the dough for 5 minutes until smooth and velvety. Wrap in cling film to prevent the dough drying out and leave to rest for 15-20 minutes.

VARIATIONS

TOMATO PASTA: Add 10 ml (2 tsp) concentrated tomato purée per egg. Add to the flour well with the eggs.
SPINACH PASTA: Add 50 g (2 oz) frozen chopped spinach, thawed, per egg. Squeeze the spinach of as much moisture as possible. Add to the flour well with the eggs.
GARLIC AND HERB PASTA: Add 1 crushed garlic clove plus 20 ml (4 tsp) finely chopped fresh herbs per egg. Add to the flour well with the eggs.

ROLLING OUT USING A PASTA MACHINE

Most pasta machines work in the same way and the following method should apply, but do refer to the manufacturer's instructions for your particular model.

1. Slice off about one fifth of the dough. Re-wrap the rest in cling film so it does not dry out. Flatten the dough slightly by hand to fit in the machine. Starting with the machine set to roll at the thickest setting (ie rollers widest apart) pass the dough through the machine.

2. Fold the strip of dough in three, rotate and pass through the machine again. Repeat the folding and, with the rollers at this widest setting, pass the dough through once more. The dough should now be smooth and of an even thickness.

3. Adjust the setting of the rollers by one notch. Guide the dough through the machine using the hands but do not pull the dough or it may drag and tear; let the machine dictate the pace.

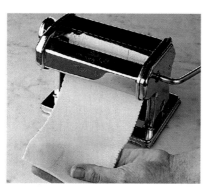

4. Pass the dough through the machine once at each narrower setting, working through to the thinnest possible. Don't be tempted to skip a setting in order to save time, or the dough may drag and tear. The dough should be gradually rolled out to a very thin large sheet. See drying and cutting (page 8-9). Repeat with remaining dough.

ROLLING OUT BY HAND

1. On a clean (not floured) surface, roll out one third of the dough to a 5 mm (¼ inch) thickness.

2. Lift the dough from the surface and rotate 45°. The dough should 'cling' (not stick) to the surface; this helps in the stretching process.

3. Continue rolling, lifting and rotating until the dough is very thin. Repeat with remaining dough.

ALLOWING PASTA TO DRY

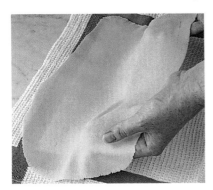

If you are making lasagne or stuffed pastas, such as ravioli or raviolini, the rolled pasta should be used immediately. Otherwise, drape the dough on a clean tea towel and leave to dry for 5-10 minutes before cutting. This makes it easier to cut and prevents the strands of pasta sticking together. Do not over-dry.

CUTTING PASTA RIBBONS BY MACHINE

Most pasta machines have tagliatelle and spaghetti cutter attachments. Do check with the instructions for your particular machine.

I. To cut tagliatelle, fit the appropriate attachment to the machine. Cut the pasta sheets into 25-30 cm (10-12 inch) lengths. Pass these through the machine.

2. To cut spaghetti, fit the appropriate attachment to the machine. Cut the pasta sheets into lengths and pass through the machine as for tagliatelle.

CUTTING PASTA RIBBONS BY HAND

I. Loosely roll up sheets of pasta, like a Swiss roll.

2. Using a large sharp knife, cut into slices, the thickness depending on the pasta ribbons required. Use the following as a guide:
linguine – 5 mm (¼ inch);
tagliatelle – 8 mm (⅓ inch);
pappardelle – 2 cm (¾ inch).

3. Carefully unravel the pasta ribbons by hand.

4. Alternatively cut pappardelle from a pasta sheet. Using a pastry wheel, plain or fluted, cut into strips about 2 cm (¾ inch) wide.

LASAGNE AND CANNELLONI

Cut the rolled-out sheets of pasta into rectangles, measuring about 10 x 15 cm (4 x 6 inches), using a sharp knife or a pastry wheel.

SHAPING RAVIOLINI

1. Take a sheet of pasta. Using a 7.5 cm (3 inch) metal fluted round cutter, stamp out circles of dough.

2. Spoon a small heap of stuffing onto each pasta circle. Moisten the edges with a little water.

3. Fold each filled pasta circle in half to give a semi-circular shape, enclosing the filling. Press the edges together lightly to seal.

SHAPING RAVIOLI

1. Take a sheet of pasta 10-12 cm (4-5 inches) wide. Spoon heaped teaspoons of stuffing at 6 cm (2½ inch) intervals along the strip.

2. Using a pastry brush, lightly moisten the edges and between the stuffing with a little water.

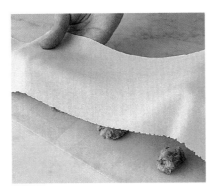

3. Lift another sheet of rolled-out pasta over the top and position carefully.

4. Use your fingers to press along the edges of the pasta and between the stuffing to seal.

5. Using a fluted pastry wheel or sharp knife, cut between the stuffing at 6 cm (2½ inch) intervals and cut neatly along the long edges.

NOTE: Until you are confident it is best not to have large quantities of dough rolled out and drying at one time. Fill pasta shapes in small quantities so the dough doesn't become over-dry and brittle.

PASTA WITH MUSSELS AND RED PESTO

This homemade red pesto makes a quick and delicious pasta sauce in its own right, tossed into hot pasta ribbons, with or without a little cream or fromage frais. In this recipe it's combined with freshly steamed mussels. For optimum effect, serve on plain egg pasta to show off the vivid orange colours, and remember to leave a few mussels in their shells as a garnish.

SERVES 4-6

1 kg (2 lb) mussels in shells
1 shallot or small onion
90 ml (3 fl oz) dry white wine
30 ml (2 tbsp) chopped fresh
   parsley
400 g (14 oz) dried ribbon
   pasta, eg tagliatelle
40 g (1½ oz) butter
RED PESTO
2 garlic cloves, peeled
25 g (1 oz) walnuts
40 g (1½ oz) basil leaves
   (from 3 basil plants)
60 ml (4 tbsp) finely chopped
   sun-dried tomatoes in oil
75 ml (5 tbsp) extra-virgin
   olive oil
30 ml (2 tbsp) pine nuts
75 ml (5 tbsp) freshly grated
   Parmesan cheese
salt and pepper
TO SERVE
Parmesan cheese

PREPARATION TIME
20 minutes
COOKING TIME
About 10 minutes
FREEZING
Not suitable

895-595 CALS PER SERVING

1. First make the red pesto: roughly chop the garlic cloves and walnuts. Put them into a food processor or blender with the basil leaves, chopped sun-dried tomatoes plus 30 ml (2 tbsp) of their oil, the olive oil and pine nuts. Process until fairly smooth and creamy.

2. Transfer the paste to a bowl and stir in the grated Parmesan. Season with a little salt and lots of pepper. (Note that the sun-dried tomatoes and cheese are quite salty). Set aside.

3. Wash the mussels thoroughly in plenty of cold water, scrubbing the shells, and remove the beards. Discard any mussels which do not close when tapped firmly. Drain well. Peel and chop the shallot or onion.

4. Place the mussels in a large saucepan with the shallot or onion, wine and parsley. Season lightly. Cook over a high heat until the liquid comes to the boil, then cover with a tight-fitting lid and cook for 3-4 minutes until the mussels are steamed open. Drain the mussels and discard any which have not opened.

5. Remove most of the mussels from their shells, then put all of them into a bowl and set aside.

6. Meanwhile, cook the pasta in a large pan of boiling salted water until 'al dente', or according to packet instructions. Drain well.

7. To serve, transfer the red pesto to a large saucepan. Warm gently on a low heat. Add the mussels to the pan and heat *very gently*. Remove from the heat and stir in the butter. Add the pasta to the pan and toss to mix. Serve at once, with freshly grated Parmesan.

NOTE: You can prepare the red pesto up to 1 week in advance and store it in a jar – topped with a layer of olive oil to seal in the flavours.

TECHNIQUE

As you clean the mussels, pull away the stringy beard from each shell.

SPAGHETTI WITH CLAMS

Versions of this classic pasta dish abound, some with tomato, some without, but all with fresh clams, wine, garlic and parsley. I like the addition of tomato but not so much as to dominate the sauce – the clams should be the main featuring ingredient! Serve with some good flavoured bread for soaking up the last of the sauce.

SERVES 4-6

700 g (1½ lb) venus or baby
    clams in shells
3 garlic cloves, peeled
2.5 ml (½ tsp) dried chilli
    flakes
350 g (12 oz) plum
    tomatoes (or other
    flavourful tomatoes)
75 ml (5 tbsp) extra-virgin
    olive oil
100 ml (3½ fl oz) dry white
    wine
salt and pepper
400 g (14 oz) dried spaghetti
30 ml (2 tbsp) chopped fresh
    parsley
40 g (1½ oz) butter

PREPARATION TIME
15 minutes
COOKING TIME
About 8 minutes
FREEZING
Not suitable

685-460 CALS PER SERVING

1. Wash the clams in plenty of cold water and scrub the shells with a small brush. Leave to soak in a bowl of fresh cold water for 10 minutes, then rinse again and drain well. Discard any clams which do not close if their shells are tapped firmly.

2. Finely chop the garlic cloves and crush the chilli flakes; set aside. Immerse the tomatoes in a bowl of boiling water for 30 seconds, then remove with a slotted spoon and peel away their skins. Halve the tomatoes, deseed and chop the flesh.

3. Heat the olive oil in a large frying pan (large enough to hold and toss the spaghetti later). Add the chopped garlic and crushed chilli and cook over a medium high heat for 2 minutes; do not let the garlic brown. Stir in the chopped tomatoes and wine.

4. Add the clams in their shells to the pan. Season with salt and pepper, stir well and bring to the boil. Cover with a tight-fitting lid and cook for 2-3 minutes to steam open the clams. Remove from the heat; discard any clams which have not opened.

5. Meanwhile, cook the spaghetti in a large pan of boiling salted water until almost ready, but not quite 'al dente' (about 1 minute less than the cooking time). Drain thoroughly.

6. Return the clam sauce to the heat and stir in the parsley. Add the drained spaghetti and cook for 1 minute; the pasta should finish its cooking in the clam juices. Add the butter, toss lightly and serve at once.

VARIATIONS

When fresh clams are not available, use jars or cans of clams in their shells, available from Italian delicatessens and larger supermarkets. Drain thoroughly before use, and include a few chopped anchovy fillets to taste.

Alternatively, replace the clams with 1 kg (2 lb) fresh mussels in their shells.

TECHNIQUE

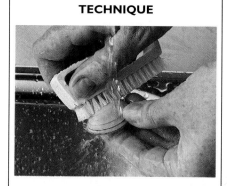

Scrub the clam shells thoroughly under cold running water to remove any grit, weed and barnacles.

PASTA WITH SCALLOPS AND GRILLED PEPPER PURÉE

Grilled pepper purée makes a superb pasta sauce – here its sweet smokiness enhances succulent grilled scallops. You could grill a red chilli along with the red peppers for an extra 'kick' if you like. Either way, serve with bread – preferably Italian olive bread – for soaking up the juices.

SERVES 4-6

4 red peppers

6 unpeeled garlic cloves

450 g (1 lb) shelled medium
  scallops

75 ml (5 tbsp) extra-virgin
  olive oil

5 ml (1 tsp) paprika

coarse sea salt and pepper

400 g (14 oz) dried ribbon
  pasta, eg tagliatelle or
  pappardelle

45 ml (3 tbsp) chopped fresh
  parsley

15 ml (1 tbsp) balsamic
  vinegar or lemon juice

60 ml (4 tbsp) freshly grated
  Parmesan cheese

TO GARNISH

parsley sprigs

PREPARATION TIME
20 minutes
COOKING TIME
35 minutes
FREEZING
Suitable: Red pepper purée only

780-520 CALS PER SERVING

1. Preheat the grill to hot. Place the whole peppers and unpeeled garlic cloves on the grill rack and grill, turning from time to time, until the peppers are blackened and blistered all over. This will take about 20 minutes, by which time the garlic cloves will be soft and tender in their papery skins. Allow to cool slightly.

2. Holding them over a bowl to catch the juices, peel the peppers, then remove the core and seeds. Peel the garlic. Chop the peppers roughly and put in a food processor with the garlic. Process for a few seconds to give a coarse purée; set aside.

3. Thread the scallops on to wooden skewers. Line the grill pan with foil to catch the juices. Brush the scallops with 30 ml (2 tbsp) of the olive oil and sprinkle with the paprika. Season liberally with sea salt and pepper. Grill for 4-5 minutes, turning once halfway through cooking, until just firm. Remove the scallops from their skewers and slice if large.

4. Cook the pasta in a large pan of boiling salted water until 'al dente', or according to packet instructions.

5. Meanwhile, transfer the pepper purée to a large frying pan. Heat gently, then stir in the scallops and the juices from the grill pan. Cook over a gentle heat for 1 minute, then stir in the parsley and balsamic vinegar or lemon juice. Remove from the heat.

6. Drain the pasta thoroughly in a colander and return to the pan. Add the remaining 45 ml (3 tbsp) olive oil and toss to mix. Add the scallops in pepper sauce and toss again lightly. Serve at once, sprinkled with the Parmesan and garnished with parsley.

NOTE: Do not be deterred by the quantity of garlic in this recipe. Grilling whole cloves until soft gives them a mild and creamy flavour.

TECHNIQUE

Grilling the scallops on skewers makes it easier to turn them. Remove and slice if large after cooking.

SHELLFISH PASTA WITH ROASTED CHERRY TOMATOES

Roasting tomatoes is a wonderful way of intensifying their flavour. Here the process is successfully applied to cherry tomatoes, to concentrate the natural sweetness they already have. The resulting deep red, soft little tomatoes are tossed into pasta – with roasted onions and seafood cooked in white wine with garlic and herbs. The result tastes as good as it looks!

SERVES 4-6

4 medium-small onions
450 g (1 lb) cherry tomatoes
75 ml (5 tbsp) extra-virgin olive oil
15 ml (1 tbsp) chopped fresh thyme
salt and pepper
1 kg (2 lb) mussels in shells
12 large raw prawns
450 g (1 lb) squid
3-4 garlic cloves, peeled
175 ml (6 fl oz) dry white wine
few parsley stalks
400 g (14 oz) dried spaghetti
TO GARNISH
chopped fresh parsley

PREPARATION TIME
30 minutes
COOKING TIME
1-1¼ hours
FREEZING
Not suitable

760-505 CALS PER SERVING

1. Preheat the oven to 200°C (400°F) Mark 6. Peel the onions and cut each one into 6 wedges, leaving the root end intact. Arrange in one layer in a roasting tin. Halve the cherry tomatoes and arrange cut side up in tin. Drizzle over 45 ml (3 tbsp) of the olive oil and sprinkle with thyme, salt and pepper. Roast in the oven for 1-1¼ hours until the onions are tender; the tomatoes will be soft.

2. Meanwhile, prepare the shellfish. Scrub and debeard the mussels, discarding any which do not close when firmly tapped. Wash the prawns but leave them whole. Clean and slice the squid.

3. About 20 minutes before serving, heat 30 ml (2 tbsp) oil in a large saucepan. Roughly slice the garlic, add to the pan and cook over a medium heat for 1 minute. Add the wine and parsley stalks, bring to the boil and cook for 2 minutes.

4. Add the prawns to the pan and cook gently, covered, for 2 minutes. Add the squid and cook for a further 1-2 minutes until both are cooked. Transfer with a slotted spoon to a plate; set aside.

5. Add the mussels to the pan, cover and cook for 3-4 minutes, shaking the pan frequently, until they open. Strain, reserving the liquid but discarding the garlic and parsley. Discard any mussels which have not opened. Return all cooked shellfish and the strained liquor to the pan.

6. Meanwhile, cook the pasta in a large pan of boiling salted water until almost 'al dente', about 1 minute less than packet instructions. Drain thoroughly, then return to the pan. Add the shellfish and cooking liquor, toss to mix and heat through gently for 1 minute.

7. Add the roasted onion and cherry tomato mixture to the pan and toss lightly. Adjust the seasoning and serve at once, sprinkled with chopped parsley.

TECHNIQUE

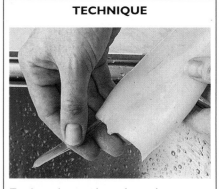

To clean the squid pouch, wash thoroughly under cold running water and pull out the transparent 'quill'.

PASTA WITH PRAWNS, MUSHROOMS AND WINE

I love the effect of 'butterflying' the prawn tails so they curl prettily as they cook, and it's very easy to do. Not only is it decorative, this technique also enables the sauce to get right through to the prawn flesh. If you need to save time, however, you can omit this stage – the dish will still taste good.

SERVES 4-6

15 g (½ oz) dried porcini
   mushrooms
16 large raw prawn tails in
   shells, about 450 g (1 lb)
   total weight
4 tomatoes
1 onion
25 g (1 oz) butter
60 ml (4 tbsp) extra-virgin
   olive oil
2 garlic cloves, crushed
150 ml (¼ pint) dry white
   wine
400 g (14 oz) large dried
   pasta shapes, eg shells,
   pipes or twists
salt and pepper
30 ml (2 tbsp) chopped fresh
   parsley
tarragon leaves to garnish
   (optional)

PREPARATION TIME
30 minutes, plus 20 minutes
soaking time
COOKING TIME
12-15 minutes
FREEZING
Not suitable

675-450 CALS PER SERVING

1. Put the dried mushrooms in a small bowl and cover with 150 ml (¼ pint) boiling water. Leave to soak for 20 minutes then drain, reserving the liquor, but take care to exclude any grit. Rinse the mushrooms and chop fairly finely.

2. 'Butterfly' the prawns by snipping lengthwise almost in half from head to tail, leaving the tail end intact. Set aside.

3. Immerse the tomatoes in boiling water for 30 seconds, cool slightly, then peel. Halve and deseed the tomatoes, then dice the flesh. Peel and chop the onion.

4. Heat the butter and oil in a large frying pan. Add the onion and cook for 5 minutes, stirring frequently, until soft but not browned. Stir in the garlic and cook for a further minute, then add the prawns and mushrooms. Cook, stirring, for a few seconds, then pour in the wine and reserved mushroom liquor. Simmer for 2-3 minutes until the prawns are firm and cooked through.

5. Meanwhile, cook the pasta in a large pan of boiling salted water until 'al dente', or according to packet instructions.

6. Using a slotted spoon transfer the prawns to a plate; set aside. Continue

cooking the mushroom mixture until the liquid is reduced by half, then stir in the tomatoes. Return prawns to the pan and season with salt and pepper. Remove from the heat until the pasta is ready.

7. Drain the pasta thoroughly and transfer to a warmed large serving bowl. Gently reheat the sauce if necessary and stir in the parsley. Add to the pasta and toss lightly to mix. Serve at once, sprinkled with tarragon leaves if desired.

VARIATION

For a rich, creamy version, add 150 ml (¼ pint) double cream to the pan after removing the prawns. Reduce the liquid by half in the same way. Finish as above.

TECHNIQUE

To 'butterfly' each prawn, start at the head end and cut lengthwise through the shell and flesh until you almost reach the tail.

CRAB-FILLED PASTA SHELLS

This elegant dish is one to reserve for special occasions. Crab is my favourite shellfish and I enjoy preparing it, but you might prefer to buy quality ready-dressed crab to save time and effort. Good fishmongers and fresh fish counters in supermarkets sell ready dressed crabmeat: it must, of course, be very fresh.

SERVES 4

450 g (1 lb) prepared crabmeat (shell and claws reserved)

300 ml (½ pint) dry white wine

1 lemon grass stalk, grated

60 ml (4 tbsp) crème fraîche (optional)

20 large dried pasta shells (see note)

1 shallot, peeled

2 red chillis

15 g (½ oz) basil leaves (from 1 plant)

25 g (1 oz) butter

salt and pepper

30-45 ml (2-3 tbsp) fresh breadcrumbs

45 ml (3 tbsp) freshly grated Parmesan cheese

olive oil, for drizzling

PREPARATION TIME
30 minutes
COOKING TIME
About 30 minutes
FREEZING
Not suitable

765 CALS PER SERVING

1. Put the crab claws and shells in a saucepan with the wine, 300 ml (½ pint) water and the lemon grass. Bring to the boil, cover and simmer for 15 minutes to make a stock. Strain, then return to the pan. Boil to reduce by one third. Stir in the crème fraîche, if using. Set aside.

2. Cook the pasta in a large pan of boiling salted water until 'al dente', or according to packet instructions. Drain thoroughly in a colander. Arrange the pasta shells upside-down on a board to dry. Preheat the oven to 220°C (425°F) Mark 7.

3. Finely chop the shallot; halve, deseed and dice the chillis very finely. Shred the basil finely. Melt the butter in a large frying pan. Add the shallot and chillis and sauté over a medium heat for 4-5 minutes to soften; do not brown. Stir in the shredded basil, cook until wilted, then remove from the heat. Add the flaked crabmeat. Mix gently and season with salt and pepper to taste.

4. Fill the pasta shells with the crab mixture and place in a large baking dish. Mix together the breadcrumbs and Parmesan. Pour the reserved stock or sauce around the shells. Sprinkle the cheese and breadcrumb mixture over the crab filling and drizzle with olive oil. Cover and cook in the preheated oven for 15 minutes, removing the lid for the last 5 minutes.

5. Transfer the crab-filled shells to warmed serving plates. Spoon the sauce or reduced stock around them and serve at once.

NOTE: You need to buy the large dried pasta shells which are suitable for stuffing. These are called *conchiglioni*.

VARIATION

Omit stage 1 and replace the reduced crab stock with a sauce made by mixing 75 ml (5 tbsp) ready-made pesto and 75 ml (5 tbsp) single cream. Spoon the sauce around the stuffed shells and bake as above.

TECHNIQUE

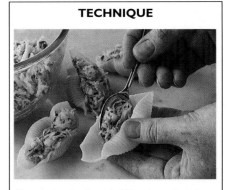

Spoon the fresh crab filling into the pre-cooked large pasta shells, or conchiglioni, using a teaspoon.

PASTA SHELLS WITH SALMON AND DILL

The pleasure of this dish lies in the unusual combination of fresh and smoked salmon with their distinctive individual qualities. It is important to add the smoked salmon at the end of cooking in order to preserve its texture and flavour. Ribbons of plain or green tagliatelle or linguine, or *paglia et fieno* – a mixture of 'straw and hay' – would be equally suitable to use.

SERVES 4-6

300 g (10 oz) fresh salmon
   fillet, skinned
125 g (4 oz) sliced smoked
   salmon
1 onion
40 g (1½ oz) butter
250 ml (8 fl oz) dry white
   wine
30 ml (2 tbsp) wholegrain
   mustard
300 ml (½ pint) extra-thick
   double cream
30-45 ml (2-3 tbsp) chopped
   fresh dill
salt and pepper
400 g (14 oz) dried pasta
   shells
TO GARNISH
dill sprigs
toasted pine nuts, for
   sprinkling (optional)

PREPARATION TIME
15 minutes
COOKING TIME
18-20 minutes
FREEZING
Not suitable

1000-670 CALS PER SERVING

1. Cut the fresh salmon fillet into 2.5 cm (1 inch) cubes. Cut the smoked salmon into strips. Set both aside. Peel and chop the onion.

2. Melt the butter in a large frying pan. Add the onion and cook over a medium heat for about 7 minutes until soft and golden. Stir in the wine and mustard and bring to the boil. Cook for 5-7 minutes until reduced by about half.

3. Stir in the cream and continue cooking for 1 minute, then lower the heat and add the fresh salmon to the pan. Cook gently for 2-3 minutes until the fish is firm. Stir in the dill and season with salt and pepper. Remove from the heat.

4. Meanwhile, cook the pasta in a large pan of boiling salted water until 'al dente', according to packet instructions. Drain thoroughly, then transfer to a warmed serving dish.

5. To serve, gently reheat the sauce if necessary. Add to the pasta with the smoked salmon strips and toss lightly to mix. Serve at once, garnished with tiny sprigs of dill and sprinkled with toasted pine nuts, if wished.

VARIATION

Substitute creamed horseradish in place of the wholegrain mustard. As the intensity of flavour varies between brands begin by adding 1 tablespoon, then taste and add more to your liking.

TECHNIQUE

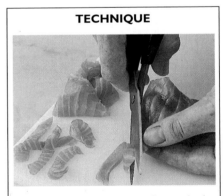

Use kitchen scissors to snip the smoked salmon slices into strips.

SMOKED FISH RAVIOLINI IN A CREAM SAUCE

These fluted semi-circular pockets are sometimes known as *agnolotti*. Here they are filled with a smoked fish, parsley and ricotta stuffing and served with a creamy sauce dotted with peas. The recipe suggests a plain egg pasta, but use spinach pasta if you prefer. For step-by-step instructions on shaping raviolini, see page 8.

SERVES 4-6

FRESH PASTA

200 g (7 oz) '00' pasta flour

2 eggs

FILLING

575 g (1¼ lb) smoked haddock fillet

15 ml (1 tbsp) olive oil

1 small onion

15 g (½ oz) butter

125 g (4 oz) ricotta cheese if available, or cream cheese

2 egg yolks

30 ml (2 tbsp) chopped fresh parsley

SAUCE

15 g (½ oz) butter

125 g (4 oz) frozen peas

300 ml (½ pint) extra-thick double cream

75 ml (5 tbsp) freshly grated Parmesan cheese

salt and pepper

TO FINISH

30 ml (2 tbsp) snipped chives

PREPARATION TIME
45 minutes
COOKING TIME
About 20 minutes
FREEZING
Suitable: Stage 5

970-650 CALS PER SERVING

1. Make the fresh pasta dough following the instructions on page 6. Wrap in cling film and leave to rest while preparing the filling. Preheat the grill to medium hot.

2. To make the filling, brush the fish all over with the olive oil and grill, skin side up to prevent the flesh from drying out, without turning, for 5-10 minutes until the flesh is firm and opaque. The exact cooking time will depend on the thickness of the fillet. Remove the skin and any bones. Flake the flesh using a fork and place in a bowl.

3. Meanwhile, peel and finely chop the onion. Melt the butter in a small frying pan. Add the onion and cook over a medium heat for about 5 minutes until soft but not browned.

4. Add the onion to the fish with the ricotta or cream cheese, egg yolks and parsley. Mix well with the fork and season with pepper; salt should not be necessary. Set aside.

5. Roll out half of the pasta dough as *thinly* as possible. Using a metal 7.5 cm (3 inch) round fluted cutter, stamp out circles of dough. Divide half of the filling between the pasta circles. Moisten the edges with a little water and fold each in half. Press the edges lightly to seal.

Repeat with the remaining pasta dough and filling. You should be able to make about 60 raviolini.

6. To make the sauce, melt the butter in a frying pan, add the peas and cook on a medium heat for 3 minutes. Stir in the cream and bring to the boil. Remove from the heat.

7. Meanwhile, cook the pasta in a large pan of boiling salted water for 2-3 minutes until 'al dente'. Drain thoroughly and transfer to warmed serving plates.

8. To serve, gently reheat the sauce and stir in the Parmesan. Season to taste. Pour over the raviolini and toss gently. Serve at once, sprinkled with chives.

TECHNIQUE

Brush the edges of the dough with a little water to help seal the semi-circular pockets on folding.

LINGUINI WITH MONKFISH AND GRILLED CHILLIS

Firm, white monkfish with capers, garlic, coriander, a little cooling mint and the bite of hot, red chilli peppers makes this an unusual, robust pasta dish. However, it's not as hot as you might imagine looking at the number of chillis in the ingredients list! Firstly, large chillis are milder than small ones, and secondly, much of their fiery heat is tempered when they are grilled and skinned.

SERVES 4-6

450 g (1 lb) monkfish, filleted

6-8 large red chillis

1 onion

3 garlic cloves

15 g (½ oz) butter

60 ml (4 tbsp) extra-virgin olive oil

30 ml (2 tbsp) capers, rinsed and drained

finely grated rind of 1 small lemon

400 g (14 oz) dried linguini or capellini

45 ml (3 tbsp) chopped fresh coriander

10 ml (2 tsp) chopped fresh mint

15 ml (1 tbsp) balsamic vinegar or lemon juice

salt and pepper

TO GARNISH

coriander leaves

PREPARATION TIME
20 minutes
COOKING TIME
About 20 minutes
FREEZING
Not suitable

605-405 CALS PER SERVING

1. Cut the monkfish fillet into thin slices and set aside.

2. Preheat the grill to hot. Grill the whole chillis, turning occasionally, until their skins are blackened and blistered all over; this will take about 10 minutes. Carefully remove and discard the skins, slit each chilli open lengthwise and rinse out the seeds under cold running water. Dry on kitchen paper. Cut the flesh lengthwise into thin strips.

3. Peel and chop the onion; peel and thinly slice the garlic.

4. Heat the butter and oil in a large frying pan. Add the onion and cook over a medium heat for 5 minutes, stirring frequently, until softened but not brown. Stir in the garlic and cook for a further minute.

5. Increase the heat to medium high and add the monkfish to the pan. Cook, stirring, for 3-4 minutes until the fish is firm and opaque. Lower the heat and stir in the capers, chilli strips and lemon rind. Remove from the heat until the pasta is ready.

6. Meanwhile, cook the pasta in a large pan of boiling salted water until 'al dente' or according to packet instructions. Drain thoroughly in a colander.

7. Heat the monkfish through gently, then remove from the heat and stir in the coriander, mint and balsamic vinegar or lemon juice. Season with salt and pepper to taste. Add the pasta and toss lightly to mix. Serve at once, garnished with coriander leaves.

VARIATION

Substitute 350 g (12 oz) peeled prawns for the monkfish reducing the cooking as follows: Do not increase the heat when adding the prawns and heat for only 1 minute before adding the chillis and lemon zest. Continue as above.

TECHNIQUE

Cook the monkfish, stirring constantly, until it is firm and opaque before adding the capers.

CHICKEN SOUP WITH GARLIC AND PARMESAN CROÛTONS

A hearty main course soup of chicken, pasta and vegetables with robust garlic and Parmesan croûtons to accompany. There are seemingly hundreds of tiny pasta shapes available for adding to soups – tiny bows, stars, hoops, alphabet letters etc – which the Italians refer to as *pastina*, or 'little pasta'. Use any one of these, according to your whim, or opt for a slightly larger shape if you prefer.

SERVES 6

1 small chicken, weighing
about 1 kg (2 lb)
300 ml (½ pint) dry white wine
few peppercorns
1-2 red chillis
2 bay leaves
2 rosemary sprigs
1 celery stalk
4 carrots
3 onions
75 g (3 oz) dried pasta shapes
1 cos lettuce
25 g (1 oz) butter
1 garlic clove, crushed
30 ml (2 tbsp) chopped fresh
parsley
salt and pepper
CROÛTONS
50 g (2 oz) butter, softened
1 garlic clove, crushed
4 thick slices white bread
45 ml (3 tbsp) freshly grated
Parmesan cheese

PREPARATION TIME
20 minutes
COOKING TIME
About 1¼ hours
FREEZING
Suitable: Stage 2

385 CALS PER SERVING

1. Put the chicken in a saucepan just large enough to contain it, with the wine, peppercorns, chillis, bay leaves and rosemary. Roughly chop the celery and 3 carrots; quarter 2 onions. Add these to the pan with about 900 ml (1½ pints) cold water to almost cover the chicken. Bring to the boil, lower the heat, cover and simmer gently for 1 hour.

2. Leave to cool slightly, then transfer the chicken to a plate and strain the stock. When cool enough to handle remove the chicken from the bone and tear into bite-sized pieces; set aside.

3. Return the stock to the pan. Bring back to the boil, add the pasta and cook for 5 minutes. Preheat the oven to 200°C (400°F) Mark 6.

4. Meanwhile, cut the remaining carrot into fine matchsticks. Peel and chop the remaining onion. Finely shred the lettuce.

5. Melt the butter in a clean pan. Add the onion and garlic and cook for 5 minutes until softened. Add the carrot and cook for 2 minutes. Add the stock and pasta and cook for 5 minutes, then stir in the chicken pieces, lettuce and parsley. Heat gently, stirring, until the lettuce has wilted. Season to taste.

6. Meanwhile, make the croûtons. Mix together the butter and garlic in a small bowl. Remove the crusts from the bread, then spread with the garlic butter and sprinkle with Parmesan. Cut into squares and place on a lightly greased baking sheet, spacing them a little apart. Bake in the oven for 8-10 minutes until crisp and golden brown.

7. Serve the chicken soup in warmed bowls, accompanied by the hot garlic and Parmesan croûtons.

NOTE: For the croûtons, cut thick slices from a whole loaf rather than use ready-sliced bread.

TECHNIQUE

To make the croûtons, spread thick slices of bread liberally with garlic butter and sprinkle with Parmesan before cutting into cubes and baking.

TAGLIATELLE WITH CHICKEN AND COURGETTES

Buttery chicken is flavoured with garlic, ginger and chilli and tossed into pasta ribbons with melting courgettes and fresh herbs. Serve the dish on its own or accompanied by a crisp, mixed leaf salad – such as rocket and chicory, or radicchio and frisée – tossed in a light, creamy dressing.

SERVES 4

3.5 cm (1½ inch) piece fresh
    root ginger
3 garlic cloves, peeled
3 red chillis
4 boneless chicken breasts,
    skinned
65 g (2½ oz) butter
coarse sea salt and pepper
2 small courgettes
45 ml (3 tbsp) chopped fresh
    coriander or tarragon
15 ml (1 tbsp) chopped fresh
    parsley
400 g (14 oz) tagliatelle

PREPARATION TIME
15 minutes
COOKING TIME
About 35 minutes
FREEZING
Not suitable

640 CALS PER SERVING

1. Preheat the oven to 190°C (375°F) Mark 5. Peel and grate the root ginger. Chop the garlic finely. Halve, deseed and chop the chillis. Arrange the chicken breasts in one layer on a large piece of foil and sprinkle with the ginger, garlic and chillis. Dot with 25 g (1 oz) of the butter and season with salt and pepper.

2. Wrap the foil tightly to form a parcel and place on a baking sheet. Bake in the oven for 30 minutes or until the chicken is tender and cooked through.

3. Meanwhile, thinly slice the courgettes. Melt the remaining butter in a large frying pan. Add the courgettes and cook over a medium heat, stirring frequently, for 4-5 minutes until tender and just beginning to brown. Stir in the herbs and cook briefly. Remove from the heat.

4. About 5 minutes before the chicken will be ready, cook the pasta in a large pan of boiling salted water until 'al dente' or according to packet instructions.

5. When the chicken is cooked, carefully lift out, retaining the juices in the foil parcel. Cut the chicken into slices or cubes and return to the foil.

6. Drain the pasta and return to the pan. Add the chicken with its juices and the courgettes, butter and herbs. Toss lightly to mix. Adjust the seasoning to taste and serve at once.

VARIATION

Replace the chicken breasts with 450 g (1 lb) salmon fillet, skinned. Use only 2 garlic cloves. Cook the salmon in the parcel as above but reduce the cooking time to 20-25 minutes; the fish should be opaque, firm and flake easily.

TECHNIQUE

Baking the chicken in a foil parcel with flavouring ingredients keeps it moist and tender and seals in the juices.

PASTA WITH CHICKEN LIVERS AND PEAS

The smooth rich flavour of chicken livers is well balanced by the simplicity of plain cooked pasta. Here the livers are served in a wine sauce, topped with a spoonful of fromage frais and a sprinkling of crisply cooked pancetta or bacon strips. Peas or petits pois add their fresh sweetness to the dish.

SERVES 4-6

450 g (1 lb) chicken livers

3 shallots or 1 small onion

1 garlic clove

50 g (2 oz) smoked
   pancetta, in one piece, or
   smoked streaky bacon

40 g (1½ oz) butter

30 ml (2 tbsp) finely
   chopped fresh parsley

120 ml (4 fl oz) dry white
   wine

50 g (2 oz) frozen petits pois
   or peas, thawed

90 ml (6 tbsp) fromage frais
   (40% fat)

salt and pepper

400 g (14 oz) tagliatelle,
   preferably fresh plain or
   garlic and herb pasta

TO FINISH

20 ml (4 tsp) fromage frais

PREPARATION TIME
15 minutes
COOKING TIME
About 20 minutes
FREEZING
Not suitable

690-460 CALS PER SERVING

1. Rinse and drain the chicken livers. Chop them roughly, discarding any fibrous bits. Peel and chop the shallots or onion and crush the garlic.

2. Cut the rind from the pancetta or bacon and slice into small strips or 'lardons'. Cook in a small pan, without any extra fat, over a medium heat for 4-5 minutes until the pancetta or bacon is lightly browned and just crisp. Transfer to a plate; set aside.

3. Melt 25 g (1 oz) of the butter in a large frying pan. Add the shallots or onion and garlic and cook over a medium heat, stirring frequently, for 5 minutes until softened, but not brown.

4. Increase the heat and add the chicken livers to the pan. Cook, stirring frequently, for 4-5 minutes until browned and sealed. Stir in the parsley and wine and continue cooking over a high heat for 3 minutes or until about two thirds of the liquid has evaporated, leaving a rich sauce. Stir in the peas.

5. Meanwhile, cook the tagliatelle in a large pan of boiling salted water until 'al dente'. For dried pasta cook according to the packet instructions. If using fresh pasta cook for 2-4 minutes only.

6. Drain the pasta thoroughly and return to the pan with the remaining 15 g (½ oz) butter. Toss to mix.

7. Add the fromage frais to the chicken livers and cook, stirring, for 2-3 minutes on a medium heat. Remove from the heat and season with salt and pepper.

8. Serve the pasta on individual plates topped with the chicken liver mixture. Add a spoonful of fromage frais to each serving and sprinkle with the reserved pancetta or bacon.

TECHNIQUE

Trim away any membranes and tubes from the chicken livers before cutting them into smaller pieces.

PAPPARDELLE WITH FRAZZLED PROSCIUTTO AND ASPARAGUS

If you enjoy the distinctive flavour of prosciutto or Parma ham eaten raw as a simple starter or lunch with fresh melon, pears or figs, try including it in cooked dishes too. It's good on thin, crisp pizzas and – as in this recipe – wafer-thin slices are delicious 'frazzled' in a pan with olive oil. For a less substantial dish you can omit the goat's cheese from this recipe.

SERVES 4-6

350 g (12 oz) frozen young
   broad beans, thawed
3 shallots
2 garlic cloves
350 g (12 oz) asparagus
90 ml (6 tbsp) extra-virgin
   olive oil
175 g (6 oz) prosciutto or
   Parma ham, in thin slices
400 g (14 oz) dried
   pappardelle or other
   pasta ribbons
45 ml (3 tbsp) chopped fresh
   parsley
salt and pepper
300 g (10 oz) goat's cheese
   log, with rind

PREPARATION TIME
30 minutes
COOKING TIME
About 12 minutes
FREEZING
Not suitable

850-565 CALS PER SERVING

1. Slip the broad beans out of their waxy outer skins into a bowl and set aside. Peel and finely chop the shallots; crush the garlic.

2. Trim the asparagus, discarding any woody parts of the stems. Cook in shallow boiling water for about 4 minutes until almost tender. Drain and refresh under cold running water. Cut into 5 cm (2 inch) lengths; set aside.

3. Heat the oil in a large frying pan. Add the prosciutto, in batches if necessary, and fry over a high heat for a few seconds. Lift out on to a plate; set aside.

4. Add the shallots and garlic to the frying pan and cook gently for 5 minutes to soften; do not allow to brown. Increase the heat to medium and add the broad beans. Cook, stirring, for 4 minutes.

5. Cook the pasta in a large pan of boiling salted water until 'al dente' or according to packet instructions.

6. Meanwhile, preheat the grill to hot. Add the asparagus to the frying pan with the parsley. Cook, stirring, for 2 minutes, then return the prosciutto to the pan. Season with salt and pepper. Remove from heat.

7. Meanwhile, cut the goat's cheese into slices and arrange on a lightly greased baking sheet. Grill for 3-4 minutes until lightly browned.

8. Drain the pasta thoroughly. Gently reheat the prosciutto mixture if necessary, then lightly toss with the pasta in the large pan. Arrange on serving plates and top with the grilled goat's cheese. Serve at once.

VARIATION

Replace the broad beans with 75 g (3 oz) fresh rocket. Add to the pan with the asparagus and parsley.

TECHNIQUE

Fry the prosciutto slices, a few at a time, in the olive oil until crinkled and crisp.

RIGATONI BAKED WITH SPICY SAUSAGE

You can use any good quality spicy sausages for this recipe, but – if at all possible – buy Italian-style uncooked sausages 'loose' from a good butcher or delicatessen, rather than prepacked ones. Prepare the sauce in advance if you wish, but don't toss with the pasta until ready for the oven, otherwise the pasta will become soggy.

SERVES 4-6

45 ml (3 tbsp) extra-virgin
   olive oil
350 g (12 oz) uncooked
   spicy sausage
1 onion
2 garlic cloves
12 black olives
5 sun-dried tomatoes
90 ml (3 fl oz) dry white wine
30 ml (2 tbsp) chopped fresh
   oregano
15 ml (1 tbsp) chopped fresh
   parsley
Two 397 g (14 oz) cans plum
   tomatoes
salt and pepper
400 g (14 oz) dried rigatoni
15 g (½ oz) butter
175 g (6 oz) mozzarella
   cheese (preferably
   smoked), diced
50 g (2 oz) Parmesan
   cheese, in one piece
oregano sprigs, to garnish

PREPARATION TIME
15-20 minutes
COOKING TIME
30-35 minutes
FREEZING
Not suitable

1000-670 CALS PER SERVING

1. Heat 15 ml (1 tbsp) of the oil in a large frying pan, then add the sausage, cut into lengths to fit the pan, if necessary. Fry on a medium high heat for 4-5 minutes, turning frequently, until lightly browned. Transfer to a plate and cut into slices. Set aside.

2. Peel and chop the onion and garlic. Slice the olives from their stones; dice the sun-dried tomatoes. Add the remaining oil to the frying pan. Stir in the onion and garlic and cook over a medium heat for 5 minutes, until softened but not browned. Return the sliced sausage to the pan and add the wine and herbs. Increase the heat and cook for 3-4 minutes until about two thirds of the wine has evaporated.

3. Stir in the canned tomatoes and their juice, breaking them up with a wooden spoon. Add the sun-dried tomatoes and olives. Cook, uncovered, over a medium heat for 15-20 minutes until the tomatoes are pulp-like; do not reduce the sauce too much. Season to taste.

4. Meanwhile, preheat the oven to 200°C (400°F) Mark 6. Cook the rigatoni in a large pan of boiling salted water until almost 'al dente', or for about 2 minutes less time than packet instructions. Drain thoroughly.

5. Butter a baking dish large enough to hold the pasta and sauce. Transfer the pasta to the dish and toss with the sauce. Scatter the mozzarella over the rigatoni. Using a potato peeler 'shave' the Parmesan cheese over the top. Bake near the top of the oven for about 15 minutes, until piping hot. Serve at once, garnished with oregano sprigs.

VARIATION

Use cooked sausages, such as chorizo, instead of raw ones. Omit stage 1. Simply slice the sausages and add at stage 2.

TECHNIQUE

Toss the rigatoni with the sauce just before baking. The pasta will finish cooking in the sauce.

PUMPKIN RAVIOLI WITH BUTTER AND HERBS

Pumpkin makes a wonderful filling for pasta with its velvet texture, rich golden colour and distinctive nutty flavour. Here it is baked in the oven before mashing; boiling is a short cut to be avoided as it makes the pumpkin flesh too wet. Other firm-fleshed squash, such as butternut or acorn, can be used.

SERVES 4

PASTA DOUGH
200 g (7 oz) '00' pasta flour
2 eggs
FILLING
450 g (1 lb) wedge pumpkin
30 ml (2 tbsp) olive oil
75 g (3 oz) prosciutto or
 Parma ham, finely chopped
50 g (2 oz) provolone or
 Parmesan cheese, finely
 grated
20 ml (1½ tbsp) chopped
 fresh basil
20 ml (1½ tbsp) chopped
 fresh parsley
1 egg yolk
freshly grated nutmeg, to
 taste
30 ml (2 tbsp) double cream
salt and pepper
TO SERVE
25 g (1 oz) butter, melted
chopped fresh herbs, to taste

PREPARATION TIME
About 45 minutes
COOKING TIME
1¼ hours
FREEZING
Suitable: Stage 5

490 CALS PER SERVING

1. For the filling, preheat the oven to 190°C (375°F) Mark 5. Brush the pumpkin flesh with the oil and bake in the oven for about 1 hour until soft.

2. Meanwhile, make the pasta dough following the instructions on page 6. Wrap in cling film and leave to rest for 20 minutes.

3. Allow the cooked pumpkin to cool slightly, then scrape the flesh into a large bowl and mash until smooth. Add all the other filling ingredients and mix well.

4. If rolling out the pasta dough by hand, divide in half and roll into 2 sheets. If using a pasta machine, roll manageable portions into strips (see page 7). Either way, roll out as thinly as possible. Keep covered with cling film to prevent them drying out.

5. Take a strip of pasta 10-12 cm (4-5 inches) wide. Spoon on heaped tea-spoonfuls of stuffing at 6 cm (2½ inch) intervals. Brush the edges and between the stuffing with a little water. Cover with another sheet of pasta and press along the edges and between the stuffing to seal. Cut between the stuffing at 6 cm (2½ inch) intervals and cut neatly along the long edges. Repeat to use all of the pasta and stuffing, to make 20-24 ravioli.

6. Bring a large saucepan of salted water to the boil. Cook the ravioli in batches for about 3 minutes until the sealed edges are 'al dente'. Drain thoroughly and transfer to a warmed serving dish. Add the butter, herbs, salt and pepper. Toss lightly to coat and serve at once.

NOTE: For detailed step-by-step instructions on shaping ravioli, see page 8.

VARIATION

For a vegetarian version, replace the prosciutto in the filling with 50 g (2 oz) walnuts, finely chopped.

TECHNIQUE

Spoon heaped teaspoonfuls of stuffing at 6 cm (2½ inch) intervals along the strip of pasta.

SPAGHETTI WITH LAMB RAGU

A good ragu needs long, slow cooking. The sauce is reduced to a flavoursome concentrate and the meat become meltingly tender. Tossed with perfectly cooked spaghetti and freshly grated Parmesan cheese this is real Italian comfort food, which is hard to beat.

SERVES 4-6

1 onion
2 garlic cloves
10 ml (2 tsp) fennel seeds
2 carrots
2 celery stalks
45 ml (3 tbsp) extra-virgin
   olive oil
350 g (12 oz) minced lamb
200 ml (7 fl oz) red wine
45 ml (3 tbsp) chopped fresh
   oregano
1 rosemary sprig
½ cinnamon stick
397 g (14 oz) can chopped
   tomatoes
salt and pepper
400 g (14 oz) dried
   spaghetti, fettucine or
   long fusilli
75 ml (5 tbsp) freshly grated
   Parmesan cheese

PREPARATION TIME
25 minutes
COOKING TIME
2½-3 hours
FREEZING
Suitable: Stage 4

740-495 CALS PER SERVING

1. Peel and finely chop the onion and garlic. Lightly crush the fennel seeds. Finely dice the carrots and celery.

2. Heat the oil in a saucepan. Add the onion and garlic and cook over a medium heat for 5 minutes until softened but not browned. Add the fennel seeds and cook for 1 minute, then add the carrot and celery and cook, stirring, for 2 minutes.

3. Add the lamb to the pan and cook for about 7 minutes, breaking up the pieces with a wooden spoon, until browned. Increase the heat and stir in the wine. Let bubble for 4-5 minutes until the liquid has reduced by about half.

4. Add the oregano, rosemary sprig and cinnamon to the pan with the canned tomatoes and their juice. Bring to the boil and season lightly with salt and pepper. Cook, uncovered, on a very low heat for 2½-3 hours, stirring occasionally until the lamb is meltingly tender and the oil separates from the sauce. Remove and discard the cinnamon and rosemary. Spoon off the oil, soaking up any excess with kitchen paper. Adjust the seasoning to taste.

5. Just before serving, cook the spaghetti in a large pan of boiling salted water until 'al dente' or according to packet instructions. Drain thoroughly.

6. To serve, toss the ragu with the pasta and about half of the grated Parmesan. Serve at once, sprinkled with the remaining Parmesan.

NOTE: The sauce tastes even better if it is prepared ahead, allowed to cool and left to stand for a while. Remove any fat from the surface and reheat thoroughly before serving.

VARIATION

For the classic Spaghetti alla Bolognese substitute lean minced beef for the lamb. Replace the rosemary with a few sprigs of fresh thyme.

TECHNIQUE

For the ragu, lightly crush the fennel seeds using a pestle and mortar if possible.

CANNELLONI

Don't be put off by the large numbers of garlic cloves in the recipe. Roasted whole, garlic has a much milder flavour with a delicious sweetness that goes perfectly with red meats. You can buy cannelloni tubes ready for cooking and stuffing or, as in this recipe, you can roll up lasagne sheets to encase the filling.

SERVES 4-6

about 12 sheets of lasagne
FILLING
20 unpeeled garlic cloves
**   (from 2 bulbs garlic)**
30 ml (2 tbsp) extra-virgin
**   olive oil**
15 g (½ oz) dried porcini
**   mushrooms**
3 shallots
450 g (1 lb) lean minced
**   beef**
150 ml (¼ pint) red wine
30 ml (2 tbsp) chopped fresh
**   thyme**
salt and pepper
TO FINISH
150 ml (¼ pint) single
**   cream**
30 ml (2 tbsp) sun-dried
**   tomato paste (see note on**
**   page 72)**
15 g (½ oz) butter
75 g (3 oz) provolone or
**   gruyère cheese, finely**
**   grated**
herb sprigs, to garnish

PREPARATION TIME
30 minutes
COOKING TIME
About 1 hour
FREEZING
Suitable: Stage 4

815-545 CALS PER SERVING

1. Preheat the oven to 180°C (350°F) Mark 4. Put the unpeeled but separated garlic cloves in a small roasting tin with 15 ml (1 tbsp) of the oil. Toss to coat the garlic in the oil and bake in the oven for 25 minutes until soft. Leave to cool.

2. Put the dried mushrooms in a small bowl and cover with 150 ml (¼ pint) boiling water. Leave to soak for 20 minutes then drain, reserving the soaking liquor. Rinse the mushrooms to remove any grit, then chop finely. Peel and finely chop the shallots.

3. Heat the remaining 15 ml (1 tbsp) oil in a saucepan. Add the shallots and cook over a medium heat for 5 minutes until soft. Increase the heat and stir in the beef. Cook, stirring frequently to break up the meat, until it is browned. Add the wine, mushrooms with their soaking liquor, and the thyme. Cook over a medium heat for 15-20 minutes or until most of the liquid has evaporated; the mixture should be quite moist.

4. Remove the papery skins from the garlic, then mash lightly, using a fork, to give a rough paste. Stir into the beef mixture, season with salt and pepper and set aside.

5. Cook the lasagne sheets in a large saucepan of boiling salted water until 'al dente' or according to packet instructions. Drain thoroughly in a colander, rinse with cold water and drain again.

6. Lay the lasagne sheets flat on a board or work surface. Spoon the beef mixture along one long edge and roll up to enclose the filling. Cut the tubes in half.

7. In a small bowl, mix together the cream and sun-dried tomato paste. Season with pepper. Set the oven temperature at 200°C (400°F) Mark 6.

8. Butter a shallow baking dish and arrange a layer of cannelloni in the base. Spoon over half of the tomato cream and sprinkle with half of the cheese. Arrange the remaining cannelloni on top and cover with the remaining tomato cream and cheese.

9. Cover the dish with foil and bake in the oven for 10 minutes, then uncover and bake for a further 5-10 minutes until lightly browned and hot. Serve at once, garnished with herbs.

TECHNIQUE

Spoon the beef filling along the long edge of each pasta sheet and roll up to enclose.

PASTA PRIMAVERA

Ribbon pasta perfectly offsets spring vegetables – or *primavera* as they are known in Italy – in this colourful dish. Some of the vegetables are cooked slowly until meltingly soft, sweet and buttery, while in contrast young asparagus, whole tiny carrots and sugar snap peas are cooked briefly to retain their fresh crispness.

SERVES 4-6

175 g (6 oz) fine asparagus

125 g (4 oz) sugar snap peas, topped and tailed

1 red pepper

2 celery stalks

2 courgettes

6-8 spring onions, white parts only

225 g (8 oz) carrots, preferably whole baby ones

1 small onion

50 g (2 oz) butter

400 g (14 oz) dried tagliatelle or pappardelle

300 ml (½ pint) double cream

60 ml (4 tbsp) freshly grated Parmesan cheese

salt and pepper

15 ml (1 tbsp) oil

20 ml (4 tsp) snipped chives

20 ml (4 tsp) chopped fresh chervil

20 ml (4 tsp) chopped fresh dill

PREPARATION TIME
25 minutes
COOKING TIME
About 25 minutes
FREEZING
Not suitable

950-635 CALS PER SERVING

1. Halve the asparagus spears and cook in boiling salted water for 3-4 minutes, adding the sugar snaps after 2 minutes so that both are cooked until just tender. Drain and refresh with cold water then drain again; set aside.

2. Using a potato peeler thinly pare the skin from the red pepper and discard, along with the core and seeds. Dice the red pepper, celery, courgettes and spring onions. If the carrots are tiny, baby ones, leave them whole; otherwise peel and cut them into matchsticks. Peel and chop the onion.

3. Melt the butter in a large frying pan. Add the onion and sauté over a medium heat for 7-8 minutes until soft and golden. Add the red pepper and celery and cook for 5 minutes. Stir in the courgettes, carrots and spring onions and cook for 12-15 minutes, stirring frequently, until the vegetables are tender and beginning to colour.

4. Cook the pasta in a large pan of boiling salted water until 'al dente' or according to packet instructions.

5. Meanwhile, stir the cream into the vegetables and bring to a gentle boil. Allow to bubble, stirring frequently for a few minutes until it reduces by about one third. Stir in the asparagus and sugar snaps. Add the Parmesan and heat gently. Season to taste.

6. Drain the pasta thoroughly and transfer to a warmed large serving bowl. Toss with the oil to prevent sticking. Pour the sauce over the pasta and sprinkle with the herbs. Toss well and serve at once.

NOTE: Because some of the vegetables are left whole it's best to balance the proportions with a good-sized pasta, and pappardelle ribbons do this beautifully. If you prefer to use a pasta shape, choose a large one – such as rigatoni, *cavatappi* (corkscrews), or the wonderfully named *'denti d'elephanti'* or elephant's teeth!

VARIATION

Substitute some of the vegetables: Try using fennel, broccoli florets, fresh peas or fine beans. Replace some of the herbs with 40 g (1½ oz) chopped walnuts.

TECHNIQUE

To immediately stop the cooking process and retain colour, refresh the asparagus and sugar snaps under cold running water.

TAGLIATELLE WITH PUMPKIN AND BLUE CHEESE SAUCE

This rich combination of pumpkin, cream and dolcelatte with broad pasta ribbons is best served with a simple salad and, perhaps, some good brown bread. Other firm-fleshed squashes, such as butternut or acorn squash, can be used with equally good results when pumpkin is out of season.

SERVES 4-6

350 g (12 oz) wedge pumpkin
1 garlic clove
25 g (1 oz) butter
30 ml (2 tbsp) chopped
   fresh parsley
300 ml (½ pint) extra-thick
   double cream
1.25 ml (¼ tsp) freshly
   grated nutmeg
400 g (14 oz) dried
   tagliatelle, pappardelle or
   fusilli
175 g (6 oz) dolcelatte
   cheese
salt and pepper
TO GARNISH
30 ml (2 tbsp) toasted pine
   nuts
15 ml (1 tbsp) chopped fresh
   parsley

PREPARATION TIME
15 minutes
COOKING TIME
About 12 minutes
FREEZING
Not suitable

930-620 CALS PER SERVING

1. Discard the seeds and remove the skin from the pumpkin. Grate the flesh, using a food processor with a grating attachment, or by hand. Crush the garlic clove.

2. Melt the butter in a large frying pan. Add the grated pumpkin and garlic and cook over a medium heat, stirring, for about 5 minutes, until softened. Stir in the parsley, cream and nutmeg and continue cooking for 2 minutes.

3. Cook the pasta in a large pan of boiling salted water until 'al dente' or according to packet instructions.

4. Cut the dolcelatte into small pieces and add to the sauce. Heat gently, stirring until melted. Season with salt and pepper to taste.

5. To serve, drain the pasta thoroughly in a colander and return to the pan. Add the sauce and toss well to mix. Transfer to a warmed serving bowl or plates and serve at once, sprinkled with toasted pine nuts and chopped parsley.

VARIATION

Replace the dolcelatte with 175 g (6 oz) 'Boursin' or other garlic and herb-flavoured cheese.

TECHNIQUE

The easiest way to grate the pumpkin flesh is to use a food processor fitted with a medium grating disc.

Capellini with Leeks, Peas and Saffron

Saffron adds its distinctive golden colour and inimitable flavour to this creamy vegetable and pasta dish. Serve accompanied by a crisp salad – either green and leafy, or try lightly cooked baby carrots dressed in a little vinaigrette as a pretty, vibrant alternative.

SERVES 4-6

1.25 ml (¼ tsp) saffron
   threads, crumbled
350 g (12 oz) leeks
50 g (2 oz) butter
150 g (5 oz) frozen peas,
   thawed
400 g (14 oz) dried capellini,
   paglia e fieno or spaghetti
300 ml (½ pint) extra-thick
   double cream
90 ml (6 tbsp) freshly grated
   Parmesan cheese
salt and pepper
TO GARNISH
chervil or parsley sprigs

PREPARATION TIME
10 minutes
COOKING TIME
15 minutes
FREEZING
Not suitable

925-615 CALS PER SERVING

1. Put the saffron in a small bowl, cover with 60 ml (4 tbsp) boiling water and leave to stand.

2. Thinly slice the leeks. Melt the butter in a large frying pan. Add the leeks and cook over a medium heat, stirring, for 7-8 minutes to soften. Add the peas and continue cooking for a further 3 minutes.

3. Meanwhile, cook the pasta in a large pan of boiling salted water until 'al dente', or according to packet instructions.

4. Add the saffron liquid and the cream to the leeks and peas. Heat gently until simmering. Stir in half of the Parmesan and remove from the heat. Season with salt and pepper.

5. Drain the pasta thoroughly and return to the pan. Add the sauce and toss lightly to mix. Add the remaining Parmesan cheese and toss again. Serve at once, garnished with chervil or parsley.

VARIATION

For non-vegetarians, add 225 g (8 oz) cooked peeled prawns. Add to the sauce once the pasta is cooked and reheat gently as above.

TECHNIQUE

Add the saffron, together with its soaking liquid, to the softened leeks and peas.

FRIED COURGETTE RIBBONS WITH LINGUINI

Tender courgette ribbons in a crisp, golden Parmesan crust contrast with a creamy smooth tomato sauce in this unusual pasta dish. The courgette ribbons take a little time to prepare, so to compensate the sauce is very simple and can be made ahead if preferred.

SERVES 4-6

SAUCE
1 onion
1 garlic clove
45 ml (3 tbsp) olive oil
397 g (14 oz) can chopped
   tomatoes
45 ml (3 tbsp) chopped fresh
   basil or oregano
salt and pepper
45 ml (3 tbsp) double cream
COURGETTE RIBBONS
350 g (12 oz) small courgettes
2 eggs
225 g (8 oz) dry white
   breadcrumbs
25 g (1 oz) freshly grated
   Parmesan cheese
10 ml (2 tsp) dried thyme
oil, for deep-frying
TO FINISH
400 g (14 oz) dried linguini
45 ml (3 tbsp) freshly grated
   Parmesan cheese
balsamic vinegar, to serve

PREPARATION TIME
About 30 minutes
COOKING TIME
20 minutes
FREEZING
Not suitable

850-565 CALS PER SERVING

1. First prepare the sauce. Peel and chop the onion and garlic. Heat the oil in a saucepan, add the onion and garlic and cook over a medium heat, stirring frequently, for 5 minutes, to soften. Add the tomatoes and herbs and bring to the boil. Lower the heat and simmer for 10 minutes. Season with salt and pepper.

2. Purée the sauce in a blender or food processor, then sieve the mixture back into the pan. Stir in the cream; set aside.

3. Using a vegetable peeler and pressing firmly, pare the courgettes into long 'ribbons'. Lightly beat the eggs in a shallow bowl. In a separate shallow bowl mix the breadcrumbs with the Parmesan, thyme, salt and pepper.

4. Heat the oil for deep frying. Dip the courgette ribbons, one at a time, first into the beaten egg and then into the breadcrumb mixture to coat.

5. Cook the pasta in a large pan of boiling salted water until 'al dente' or according to packet instructions.

6. Meanwhile, fry the courgette ribbons, in batches, in the hot oil for 1-2 minutes, until golden and crisp. Drain on kitchen paper then transfer to a plate and keep hot.

7. Gently reheat the tomato sauce. Drain the pasta thoroughly, then return to the pan. Add the sauce and Parmesan and toss lightly. Transfer to a warmed large shallow serving dish or individual plates. Pile the courgette ribbons on top and serve at once, accompanied by balsamic vinegar for sprinkling.

NOTE: If you do not have any balsamic vinegar, replace with lemon juice. To add colour, snip a few chives over the pasta before topping with the fried courgette ribbons.

TECHNIQUE

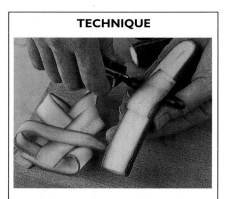

Using a potato peeler and pressing firmly, peel whole lengths of courgette to make long ribbons.

PASTA WITH CAPER SAUCE AND GRILLED CHEESE

Halloumi is a traditional Cypriot cheese with a salty flavour and a firm texture. It is wonderful for grilling or frying as it softens – rather than melts – and develops a lovely golden crust. Many supermarkets now sell halloumi, or it can be obtained from Cypriot food stores.

SERVES 4-6

2 red peppers

2 onions

2 garlic cloves

90 ml (6 tbsp) extra-virgin
   olive oil

45 ml (3 tbsp) chopped fresh
   parsley

50 g (2 oz) capers in wine
   vinegar, drained
   (drained weight)

salt and pepper

400 g (14 oz) dried penne,
   rigatoni or tagliatelle

225 g (8 oz) halloumi cheese

PREPARATION TIME
30 minutes
COOKING TIME
15 minutes
FREEZING
Not suitable

755-505 CALS PER SERVING

1. Preheat the grill to hot. Grill the whole peppers, turning occasionally until the skin is blistered and blackened all over. This will take about 20 minutes. Cool slightly then, over a bowl to catch the juices, peel away the charred skin and remove the seeds. Cut the flesh into strips and add to the bowl; set aside.

2. Meanwhile, peel and chop the onions and garlic. Heat 75 ml (5 tbsp) olive oil in a large frying pan. Add the onions and cook over a medium heat, stirring frequently, for 7-8 minutes until soft. Stir in the garlic and continue cooking for 2-3 minutes until the onion is golden. Stir in the parsley and transfer the mixture to a food processor.

3. Rinse the capers thoroughly to remove the vinegar and add to the food processor. Season with salt and pepper, then process the mixture very briefly to coarsely chop.

4. Cook the pasta in a large pan of boiling salted water until 'al dente' or according to packet instructions.

5. Meanwhile, cut the halloumi into 1 cm (½ inch) cubes. Place these in a baking tin large enough to take them in one layer. Add the remaining 15 ml (1 tbsp) olive oil and plenty of pepper. Toss to coat the cheese cubes and grill, stirring occasionally, for about 8 minutes until evenly golden on all sides.

6. Drain the pasta thoroughly and return to the large saucepan. Add the caper sauce and reserved pepper strips. Toss to mix. Transfer to a warmed serving bowl or plates and sprinkle with the grilled cheese cubes. Serve at once.

VARIATION

If halloumi is not available, use a firm goat's cheese log, cut into slices.

TECHNIQUE

Briefly process the capers with the sautéed onion and garlic mixture to chop coarsely.

SPAGHETTINI WITH WILD MUSHROOMS AND SAGE

Not everyone is lucky enough to be able to buy – or find – wild mushrooms, but cultivated large field mushrooms work well in this dish too. Whichever combination of mushrooms you choose, the dried porcini will add a superb depth of flavour to the sauce.

SERVES 4-6

15 g (½ oz) dried porcini
   mushrooms
575 g (1¼ lb) mixed fresh
   mushrooms, eg field,
   chestnut, oyster
   mushrooms, plus
   chanterelles or other wild
   types, if available
3 shallots
2-3 garlic cloves
75 ml (5 tbsp) extra-virgin
   olive oil
300 ml (½ pint) dry white
   wine
30 ml (2 tbsp) chopped fresh
   sage
30 ml (2 tbsp) chopped fresh
   parsley
salt and pepper
400 g (14 oz) dried
   spaghettini
TO SERVE
25-40 g (1-1½ oz) Parmesan
   cheese

PREPARATION TIME
25 minutes, plus soaking time
COOKING TIME
About 20 minutes
FREEZING
Not suitable

660-440 CALS PER SERVING

1. To reconstitute the dried mushrooms, put them in a small bowl and pour on 125 ml (4 fl oz) boiling water. Leave to soak for 20 minutes then drain, reserving the soaking liquor. Rinse and chop the mushrooms.

2. To prepare the fresh mushrooms, wipe them clean and trim off any roots. Slice the large field mushrooms; quarter the chestnut mushrooms; leave the oyster mushrooms and any others whole (unless they are very large). Peel and chop the shallots and garlic.

3. Heat the olive oil in a large frying pan. Add the shallots and sauté over a medium heat for 5 minutes until softened. Stir in the garlic and cook for a further 1-2 minutes.

4. Add the chopped dried mushrooms to the frying pan with the soaking liquor and the wine. Bring to the boil, then lower the heat a little and allow to bubble for 8-10 minutes until the liquid has reduced by about half.

5. Add all the fresh mushrooms, except the oyster mushrooms, to the pan with the sage. Cook for about 6 minutes until they are tender. Stir in the oyster mushrooms, parsley and seasoning. Cook for a further 2 minutes.

6. Meanwhile, cook the spaghettini in a large pan of boiling salted water until 'al dente' or according to packet instructions. Drain thoroughly and return to the pan.

7. Add the mushroom mixture to the pasta and toss lightly to mix. Adjust the seasoning and serve at once, sprinkled with shavings of Parmesan.

TECHNIQUE

To clean the fresh mushrooms, wipe them with a damp piece of absorbent kitchen paper, or cloth.

PASTA WITH MEDITERRANEAN VEGETABLES

Pasta tossed in walnut paste is a wonderful combination and a delicious dish in its own right. Topped with grilled Mediterranean vegetables it makes a gutsy, colourful dish. As an alternative you could use olive paste which is available ready-made in jars from Italian delicatessens and larger supermarkets.

SERVES 4-6

1 fennel bulb

2 small red onions, peeled

2 courgettes

1 large red pepper

6 small tomatoes

45 ml (3 tbsp) extra-virgin
   olive oil

15 ml (1 tbsp) chopped fresh
   thyme

5 ml (1 tsp) finely grated
   lemon rind

coarse sea salt and pepper

400 g (14 oz) dried
   tagliatelle

WALNUT PASTE

150 g (5 oz) walnuts,
   roughly chopped

1 garlic clove, chopped

45 ml (3 tbsp) chopped fresh
   parsley

75 ml (5 tbsp) extra-virgin
   olive oil

50 g (2 oz) ricotta or other
   soft cheese

PREPARATION TIME
25 minutes
COOKING TIME
20 minutes
FREEZING
Not suitable

950-630 CALS PER SERVING

1. Cut the fennel bulb and the onions into wedges, leaving the root ends intact. Halve the courgettes, then thinly slice lengthwise.

2. Add the fennel and onions to a large pan of boiling water, bring back to the boil and cook for 2 minutes. Add the courgette strips and cook for a further 1 minute. Drain in a colander and refresh under cold running water. Drain and set aside.

3. Preheat the grill to hot. Cut the red pepper into wide strips, discarding core and seeds; halve the tomatoes. Put the olive oil, thyme and lemon rind into a large bowl. Add all the vegetables, season and toss to coat in the flavoured oil.

4. Line the grill pan with foil. Tip in the vegetables and grill for 15-20 minutes, turning occasionally until they are tender and patched with brown.

5. Meanwhile, cook the pasta in a large pan of boiling salted water until 'al dente' or according to packet instructions.

6. Meanwhile, prepare the walnut paste. Put the walnut and garlic into a food processor and process briefly to chop finely. Add the parsley and process for 1 second. Add the oil and work to a coarse paste. Transfer to a bowl and stir in the ricotta and seasoning.

7. Drain the pasta thoroughly in a colander. Meanwhile, gently heat the walnut paste in the large pasta pan for a few seconds, then remove from the heat. Add the pasta and toss to mix. Serve at once, topped with the grilled vegetables, drizzling over any oil and juices from the grill pan.

VARIATION

Use olive rather than walnut paste. Either buy ready-made olive paste or make your own, by processing stoned olives with a chopped garlic clove, olive oil and some chopped herbs.

TECHNIQUE

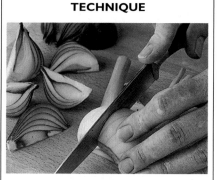

Cut the fennel bulb and onions into wedges leaving the root end attached so they do not fall apart.

VEGETARIAN LASAGNE

This vegetarian lasagne has a rich Mediterranean vegetable filling complemented by a set custard-like topping made from goat's cheese, eggs and cream. Use the mild soft young goat's cheese – Chèvre Frais – which is usually sold in tubs for this. Alternatively you can use cream cheese or curd cheese instead.

SERVES 6

4 red, orange or yellow
   peppers
2 medium aubergines
2 onions, peeled
4 garlic cloves, peeled
75 ml (5 tbsp) extra-virgin
   olive oil
45 ml (3 tbsp) chopped fresh
   oregano
75 ml (5 tbsp) red wine or
   water
90 ml (6 tbsp) sun-dried
   tomato paste (see note on
   page 72)
salt and pepper
12 sheets dried lasagne
TOPPING
350 g (12 oz) fresh soft
   goat's cheese
2 eggs
150 ml (¼ pint) single
   cream
45 ml (3 tbsp) dry white
   breadcrumbs
30 ml (2 tbsp) freshly grated
   Parmesan cheese

PREPARATION TIME
About 1 hour
COOKING TIME
40 minutes, to bake
FREEZING
Suitable: Before baking

685 CALS PER SERVING

1. Preheat the grill to hot. Grill the whole peppers, turning from time to time, until the skins are blackened and blistered all over. This will take about 20 minutes. Allow to cool slightly, then over a bowl to catch the juices, remove the skins. Chop the flesh, discarding the seeds, and set aside with the juices.

2. Meanwhile, cut the aubergines into 1 cm (½ inch) dice. Place in a colander, rinse, then sprinkle liberally with salt. Leave for 20 minutes, to extract the bitter juices. Rinse again, then blanch in boiling water for 1 minute; drain well.

3. Chop the onions; thinly slice the garlic. Heat the oil in a large saucepan. Add the onions and cook, stirring frequently, for about 8 minutes until soft and golden. Add the garlic and cook for a further 2 minutes. Add the wine and allow to bubble for 1 minute, then stir in the aubergine, oregano and sun-dried tomato paste. Cover and cook over a medium heat for 15-20 minutes, stirring frequently. Remove from the heat and stir in the grilled peppers and seasoning.

4. Preheat the oven to 190°C (375°F) Mark 5. Cook the lasagne in a large pan of boiling salted water until 'al dente' or according to packet instructions. Drain, then drop into a bowl of cold water with 30 ml (2 tbsp) oil added to prevent the sheets from sticking. Drain again and lay on a clean tea towel.

5. Oil a baking dish, measuring about 25 x 18 x 8 cm (10 x 7 x 3½ inches). Spread one third of the filling in the base and then cover with a layer of pasta, trimming to fit the dish as necessary. Add another third of the filling and cover with pasta as before. Cover with the last of the filling and arrange the remaining pasta sheets over the top.

6. To make the topping, place the goats' cheese in a bowl, add the eggs and beat well. Stir in the cream and seasoning. Pour over the lasagne and spread evenly. Sprinkle with the breadcrumbs and Parmesan, then bake for about 35-40 minutes, until heated through and lightly browned on top.

VARIATION

Replace the goat's cheese topping with 350 g (12 oz) mozzarella, cut into slices.

TECHNIQUE

Layer the filling and pasta sheets in the baking dish, trimming to fit as necessary.

TAGLIATELLE WITH BROAD BEANS, CHICORY AND CREAM

Tender, bright green broad beans and chicory are tossed in a creamy sauce, with herbs, and served with tagliatelle and Parmesan. Slipping the beans out of their waxy skins takes a little time, but it's worth the effort. If you think you'll find it tiresome, opt for the variation rather than use frozen broad beans in their skins.

SERVES 4-6

350 g (12 oz) frozen broad
   beans, thawed
1 onion
40 g (1½ oz) butter
2 heads chicory, total weight
   about 200 g (7 oz)
400 g (14 oz) dried white
   and green tagliatelle or
   freshly made tagliatelle
45 ml (3 tbsp) chopped fresh
   parsley or chervil
300 ml (½ pint) extra-thick
   double cream
60 ml (4 tbsp) freshly grated
   Parmesan cheese
salt and pepper
TO SERVE
extra herbs and Parmesan
   cheese

PREPARATION TIME
25 minutes
COOKING TIME
10 minutes
FREEZING
Not suitable

880-590 CALS PER SERVING

1. Remove the waxy outer skins from the broad beans and discard. Put the bright green beans into a bowl and set aside. Peel and finely chop the onion.

2. Melt the butter in a large frying pan. Add the onion and cook over a medium heat, stirring frequently, for 5-6 minutes until soft. Slice the chicory.

3. Cook the pasta in a large pan of boiling salted water until 'al dente' or according to packet instructions.

4. Meanwhile, add the broad beans to the onion in the frying pan and continue cooking for 2 minutes, then stir in the chicory slices and parsley or chervil. Cook for a further 2 minutes, then stir in the cream. Bring to the boil and add the grated Parmesan. Season with salt and pepper to taste.

5. Drain the pasta thoroughly and transfer to a warmed serving dish. Add the sauce and toss to mix. Serve at once, sprinkled with extra herbs and shavings of Parmesan cheese.

VARIATION

Replace the skinned broad beans with 300 g (10 oz) frozen peas. Add them to the onion with the chicory.

TECHNIQUE

Once thawed, frozen broad beans can be removed easily from their skins. Pinch one end of the skin to squeeze out the bean.

SPAGHETTI ALLA CARBONARA

This classic Italian pasta dish – with its rich smoky flavour and light, soft scrambled egg texture – is cooked as it should be, with the heat of the spaghetti setting the eggs to give a creamy sauce. If pecorino cheese is unobtainable, simply double the quantity of Parmesan.

SERVES 4-6

125-150 g (4-5 oz) smoked
  pancetta, in slices (see
  note)
1 garlic clove, peeled
30 ml (2 tbsp) extra-virgin
  olive oil
25 g (1 oz) butter
3 eggs
30 ml (2 tbsp) chopped fresh
  parsley
30 ml (2 tbsp) dry white
  wine
40 g (1½ oz) Parmesan
  cheese, grated
40 g (1½ oz) pecorino
  cheese, grated
salt and pepper
400 g (14 oz) spaghetti

PREPARATION TIME
About 15 minutes
COOKING TIME
About 7 minutes
FREEZING
Not suitable

675-450 CALS PER SERVING

1. Remove the rind from the pancetta, then cut into tiny strips. Halve the garlic. Heat the oil and butter in a heavy-based pan. Add the pancetta and garlic and cook over a medium heat for 3-4 minutes until the pancetta begins to crisp. Turn off the heat; discard the garlic.

2. Meanwhile, in a mixing bowl large enough to hold the cooked spaghetti later, beat the eggs with the parsley, wine and half of each of the cheeses. Season with salt and pepper.

3. Cook the spaghetti in a large pan of boiling salted water until 'al dente', or according to packet instructions.

4. When the spaghetti is almost cooked, gently reheat the pancetta in the pan. Drain the spaghetti thoroughly, then immediately add to the egg mixture in the bowl with the pancetta. Toss well to cook the eggs until they are creamy. Add the remaining cheeses, toss lightly and serve at once.

NOTE: Smoked pancetta is obtainable from Italian delicatessens. If it is not available use smoked bacon but you will need to increase the quantity to 175-225 g (6-8 oz) to give sufficient flavour.

VARIATION

Spaghetti with smoked salmon and scrambled eggs is prepared in a similar way. Omit the pancetta and garlic. Instead, add 125 g (4 oz) smoked salmon strips to the egg mixture at stage 2. Heat the butter and oil and add with the pasta at stage 4. Finish as above, adding the remaining cheese and tossing in the same way.

TECHNIQUE

Toss the hot pasta and pancetta with the egg mixture. The heat from the pasta will cook the eggs.

PASTA WITH SMOKED TROUT, PEPPERS AND ALMONDS

Trout with almonds is a classic combination. In this dish smoked trout fillets are flaked with grilled red peppers, as well as almonds and lots of fresh dill. It's a well flavoured dish and needs only a simple salad to offset the richness for a perfect pasta meal. A glass of chilled white wine would be good too!

SERVES 4-6

3 large red peppers

225 g (8 oz) smoked trout
  fillets

60 ml (4 tbsp) extra-virgin
  olive oil

75 g (3 oz) flaked almonds

400 g (14 oz) dried pasta
  bows, shells or pipes

45 ml (3 tbsp) chopped fresh
  dill

40 g (1½ oz) butter

salt and pepper

TO GARNISH

dill sprigs

PREPARATION TIME
20 minutes
COOKING TIME
About 30 minutes
FREEZING
Not suitable

785-525 CALS PER SERVING

1. Preheat the grill to hot. Grill the peppers whole, turning occasionally, until the skins are charred and blistered all over. This will take about 20 minutes. Allow to cool slightly, then over a bowl to catch any juices, remove the skins. Cut the peppers into thin strips, discarding the seeds.

2. Flake the smoked trout fillets. Heat the oil in a large frying pan. Add the flaked almonds and cook over a medium heat for about 3 minutes until lightly browned.

3. Meanwhile, cook the pasta in a large pan of boiling salted water until 'al dente', or according to packet instructions.

4. Add the pepper strips and any reserved juices to the almonds. Heat through for 1 minute, then stir in the chopped dill and flaked trout. Heat for 1 minute, then remove from the heat and stir in the butter; this will prevent any further cooking. Season with salt and pepper to taste.

5. To serve, drain the pasta thoroughly. Add to the smoked trout mixture and toss lightly to mix. Serve immediately, garnished with dill.

NOTE: To save time the peppers can be cut into quarters before grilling. Grill the pieces skin-side up for about 10 minutes until blistered and blackened. However, this method does not retain the sweet juices within the cooked peppers.

TECHNIQUE

When the grilled peppers are cool enough to handle, peel away the skins over a bowl to catch the juices.

FETTUCINE WITH GORGONZOLA AND SPINACH

The rich and creamy flavour of this pasta sauce belies its few simple ingredients. Use small young, tender spinach leaves if possible. Larger spinach leaves can be used, but they will need to have their stalks removed and will require shredding or rough chopping before cooking. Serve this pasta dish accompanied by some flavoured bread and, perhaps, a crisp colourful salad.

SERVES 4-6

350 g (12 oz) young leaf
   spinach
225 g (8 oz) gorgonzola
   cheese
75 ml (3 fl oz) milk
25 g (1 oz) butter
salt and pepper
400 g (14 oz) fettucine,
   tagliatelle or long fusilli
TO SERVE
freshly grated nutmeg

PREPARATION TIME
About 15 minutes
COOKING TIME
10 minutes
FREEZING
Not suitable

630-420 CALS PER SERVING

1. Wash the spinach thoroughly and remove any large stalks. Place in a clean saucepan and cook, stirring, over a medium high heat for 2-3 minutes until wilted. There is no need to add extra water – the small amount clinging to the leaves after washing provides sufficient moisture. Drain well in a colander or sieve, pressing out any excess liquid.

2. Cut the gorgonzola into small pieces. Place in a clean pan with the milk and butter. Heat gently, stirring, until melted to a creamy sauce. Stir in the drained spinach. Season to taste with pepper; salt may not be necessary because the gorgonzola is quite salty.

3. Just before serving, cook the pasta in a large pan of boiling salted water until 'al dente' or according to packet instructions. (Fresh pasta will require only 2-3 minutes cooking time.)

4. Drain the pasta thoroughly and add to the sauce. Toss well to mix. Serve at once, sprinkled with a little freshly grated nutmeg.

VARIATIONS

Add 125 g (4 oz) cooked smoked ham, cut into small dice or fine strips, to the sauce with the wilted spinach.

As an alternative to gorgonzola, make this dish with dolcelatte cheese, which will provide a milder, sweeter flavour.

TECHNIQUE

Drain the cooked spinach thoroughly, pressing it with the back of a wooden spoon to remove as much liquid as possible.

PASTA WITH COURGETTES AND BALSAMIC VINEGAR

Courgettes are cooked until meltingly soft and their sweet flavour is enlivened with the addition of balsamic vinegar. Small to medium courgettes work best in this dish and, for the pasta, choose either large ribbons, such as tagliatelle or pappardelle, or shapes such as tubes or twists.

SERVES 4-6

450 g (1 lb) courgettes

1 small onion

2 garlic cloves

75 ml (5 tbsp) extra-virgin
   olive oil

45 ml (3 tbsp) pine nuts

45 ml (3 tbsp) chopped fresh
   parsley

salt and pepper

400 g (14 oz) tagliatelle,
   pappardelle or pasta
   shapes

15-30 ml (1-2 tbsp) balsamic
   vinegar

90 ml (6 tbsp) freshly grated
   Parmesan or pecorino
   cheese

PREPARATION TIME
10 minutes
COOKING TIME
25 minutes
FREEZING
Not suitable

725-480 CALS PER SERVING

1. Cut the courgettes into thin slices. Peel and finely chop the onion and garlic.

2. Heat 30 ml (2 tbsp) olive oil in a large frying pan. Add the pine nuts and cook, stirring, over a medium high heat for 2-3 minutes until lightly browned. Transfer to a small bowl and set aside.

3. Add the remaining 45 ml (3 tbsp) oil to the pan. Stir in the onion and garlic and cook over a gentle heat for 2 minutes to soften. Add the courgettes and increase the heat. Cook, stirring, for about 4 minutes until just beginning to brown.

4. Add the parsley, seasoning and 30 ml (2 tbsp) water to the pan. Cover, lower the heat and cook gently for 15 minutes, stirring twice.

5. Meanwhile, cook the pasta in a large pan of boiling salted water until 'al dente', or according to packet instructions. (Fresh pasta ribbons will need only 2-3 minutes cooking time.)

6. Uncover the courgettes and cook for a moment or two over a high heat, stirring gently, until any excess liquid has evaporated. Remove from the heat and sprinkle with the balsamic vinegar and pine nuts.

7. Drain the pasta thoroughly and add to the courgettes with two thirds of the grated cheese. Toss to mix. Serve at once, sprinkled with the remaining grated Parmesan or pecorino.

NOTE: Balsamic vinegar can be bought at reasonable prices in many supermarkets. If you are buying it from a specialist shop you may find prices vary, depending on the maturity of the vinegar. The longer the vinegar has been matured the more concentrated the flavour, so – although more expensive – you won't need to use as much.

TECHNIQUE

Cook the courgette slices with the onion and garlic over a high heat, stirring constantly, until they are beginning to brown.

LONG FUSILLI WITH ASPARAGUS AND PARMESAN

Asparagus is a wonderful vegetable. Its presence in a dish always makes me feel I'm eating something special and extravagant – even a simple pasta dish like this! Long fusilli is a pretty and fun pasta shape – it looks like the curly cable from a telephone. But I especially like its ability to retain firmness when it is cooked and tossed in a sauce – try it with other sauces too. Serve this pasta dish with a crisp leafy salad.

SERVES 4-6

400 g (14 oz) thin asparagus
1 onion
salt and pepper
50 g (2 oz) butter
90 ml (3 fl oz) dry white wine
400 g (14 oz) dried long fusilli, tagliatelle or penne
300 ml (½ pint) extra-thick double cream
50 g (2 oz) Parmesan cheese, freshly grated

PREPARATION TIME
5 minutes
COOKING TIME
12 minutes
FREEZING
Not suitable

875-585 CALS PER SERVING

1. Trim the asparagus, discarding any tough woody bases. Pare any larger stalks with a vegetable peeler, otherwise leave whole. Peel and finely chop the onion.

2. Pour sufficient water into a frying pan to give a 2 cm (¾ inch) depth. Add a pinch of salt and bring to the boil. Add the asparagus spears and cook for 4-5 minutes until almost tender. Drain, reserving 75 ml (5 tbsp) of the cooking water. Cut the asparagus into 5 cm (2 inch) lengths and set aside.

3. Melt the butter in the frying pan. Add the onion and cook over a medium high heat for about 5 minutes until softened and beginning to colour. Stir in the asparagus and cook for 1 minute. Pour in the reserved cooking water and the wine. Cook over a high heat until almost all the liquid has evaporated.

4. Meanwhile, cook the pasta in a large pan of boiling salted water until 'al dente', or according to packet instructions.

5. Add the cream to the sauce and stir well. Heat until bubbling. Stir in half of the grated Parmesan and salt and pepper to taste.

6. Drain the pasta thoroughly and add to the sauce. Toss well to mix. Serve at once, sprinkled with the remaining Parmesan and pepper to taste.

NOTE: Pencil-slim asparagus spears work best in this dish, as larger stalks require peeling and of course yield fewer asparagus tips.

VARIATION

Add 75 g (3 oz) smoked pancetta to the sauce. Derind and cut into tiny strips or dice; add to the frying pan with the onion.

TECHNIQUE

Add the pasta to the asparagus sauce and toss well to mix before serving.

PASTA WITH TWO-TOMATO SAUCE

Made with fresh tomato and enriched with sun-dried tomato paste, this sauce is substantial enough to serve on plain pasta as a meal, but it is also good on filled pastas such as ravioli, tortelloni, cannelloni etc. Full-flavoured ripe fresh tomatoes give the best result but canned plum tomatoes are a better choice than under-ripe or flavourless fresh ones. Serve this pasta dish with flavoured bread, such as olive bread.

SERVES 4-6

1 onion

2 garlic cloves

50 g (2 oz) butter

1 kg (2 lb) ripe tomatoes, preferably plum, or two 397 g (14 oz) cans plum tomatoes with their juice

45 ml (3 tbsp) sun-dried tomato paste (see note)

2 oregano sprigs

400 g (14 oz) dried fusilli, pasta shells or penne

salt and pepper

TO SERVE

25-50 g (1-2 oz) Parmesan cheese

chopped fresh parsley, to garnish

PREPARATION TIME
About 12 minutes
COOKING TIME
25-30 minutes
FREEZING
Suitable: Sauce only

570-380 CALS PER SERVING

1. To prepare the sauce, peel and chop the onion and finely chop the garlic. Melt the butter in a saucepan, add the onion and garlic and cook over a medium low heat for about 8 minutes while preparing the tomatoes.

2. If using fresh tomatoes, first skin them. Immerse in a bowl of boiling water for 30 seconds, then drain and refresh under cold running water. Peel away the skins. Quarter the tomatoes, discard the seeds, then roughly chop the flesh. If using canned plum tomatoes, chop them roughly.

3. Add the tomatoes to the onion and garlic mixture together with the sun-dried tomato paste and oregano sprigs. Cook, uncovered, over a low heat for 25-30 minutes, stirring occasionally, until the sauce is thick and pulpy.

4. Meanwhile, cook the pasta in a large pan of boiling salted water until 'al dente' or according to packet instructions. Drain thoroughly in a colander.

5. Discard the oregano and season the sauce with salt and pepper to taste. Add the pasta and toss well to mix. Serve at once, topped with shavings of Parmesan and chopped parsley.

NOTE: You can buy sun-dried tomato paste in small jars from Italian specialist shops and some larger supermarkets, but it's also very easy to make. Simply use a food processor to purée the contents of a jar of sun-dried tomatoes in oil. I prefer to drain off some of the oil first to get a good thick paste, but don't throw it away as it has a great flavour. Return the paste to the empty jar and store in the refrigerator until required.

TECHNIQUE

Immerse the tomatoes in boiling water for 30 seconds, then drain, refresh and peel away the skins.

TAGLIATELLE WITH SAGE, PIMENTO AND GARLIC

I use canned pimento in this recipe as a really fast alternative to grilled and skinned peppers. They work quite well in the creamy sauce, lending a more mellow flavour than fresh whole peppers. If you have the time and want to use fresh peppers instead, you'll need to grill and skin three large red ones.

SERVES 4-6

1 small onion
2 garlic cloves
60 ml (4 tbsp) extra-virgin
　olive oil
400 g (14 oz) can pimento in
　brine
30 ml (2 tbsp) chopped fresh
　sage
150 ml (¼ pint) extra-thick
　double cream
75 ml (5 tbsp) freshly grated
　Parmesan cheese
salt and pepper
400 g (14 oz) green and
　plain tagliatelle
TO GARNISH
sage sprigs

PREPARATION TIME
10 minutes
COOKING TIME
About 10 minutes
FREEZING
Not suitable

775-520 CALS PER SERVING

1. Peel and finely chop the onion and garlic. Heat the oil in a large frying pan. Add the onion and garlic and cook over a medium heat for about 5 minutes until softened; do not allow to brown.

2. Drain and rinse the canned pimento, then drain well and cut into fairly small dice. Add to the frying pan with the chopped sage and continue cooking for 3 minutes. Stir in the cream and bring to a simmer, then stir in all but 15 ml (1 tbsp) of the grated Parmesan. Season with salt and pepper to taste.

3. Meanwhile, cook the pasta in a large pan of boiling salted water until 'al dente', or according to packet instructions. (Fresh pasta will require only 2-3 minutes cooking time.)

4. To serve, drain the pasta thoroughly and add to the sauce. Toss well to mix. Serve sprinkled with the remaining grated Parmesan and garnished with sage leaves.

NOTE: Extra-thick double cream is used here and in other creamy sauces as it lends the correct consistency. If you prefer to use ordinary double cream, increase the quantity by about one third and reduce the creamy sauce slightly by simmering until the desired consistency is obtained.

VARIATION

Use pasta tubes, such as rigatoni or penne, in place of the tagliatelle and add 175 g (6 oz) diced mozzarella cheese to the sauce at the end of cooking. The cheese cubes should melt softly when tossed with the hot pasta but not disappear completely into the sauce.

TECHNIQUE

As soon as the tagliatelle is cooked, drain it thoroughly in a colander before tossing with the sauce.

PAPPARDELLE WITH ARTICHOKES AND CREAM

This simple dish makes a quick and sustaining meal when served with a leafy salad or a tomato and basil salad, and some rustic bread. If you prefer, serve the sauce on finer pasta such as spaghetti or paglia e fieno.

SERVES 4-6

400 g (14 oz) dried pappardelle or tagliatelle

12 artichoke hearts, preserved in oil

2 garlic cloves, peeled

25 g (1 oz) butter

45 ml (3 tbsp) chopped fresh parsley

300 ml (½ pint) extra-thick double cream

90 ml (6 tbsp) freshly grated pecorino or Parmesan cheese

salt and pepper

PREPARATION TIME
5-10 minutes
COOKING TIME
10 minutes
FREEZING
Not suitable

835-555 CALS PER SERVING

1. Cook the pasta in a large pan of boiling salted water until 'al dente', or according to packet instructions.

2. Meanwhile, prepare the sauce. Drain the artichoke hearts and slice them thinly. Finely chop the garlic. Melt the butter in a large frying pan. Add the garlic and cook over a gentle heat for about 3 minutes to soften; do not allow to brown.

3. Add the artichokes and 30 ml (2 tbsp) of the chopped parsley to the frying pan. Cook, stirring, for 2 minutes. Stir in the cream and bring to a simmer. Stir in the grated cheese and cook for a further 1 minute. Season with salt and pepper to taste.

4. To serve, drain the pasta thoroughly in a colander. Add to the sauce and toss well to mix. Serve at once, sprinkled with the remaining chopped parsley.

NOTE: Artichoke hearts preserved in oil are available in jars from many supermarkets and are often sold 'loose' at Italian specialist shops. They are quite superior in flavour to canned artichoke hearts in brine which should not be used for this recipe.

VARIATION

Add 50-75 g (2-3 oz) roughly chopped walnuts to the sauce at the same stage as the pecorino or Parmesan cheese. If available, use 45 ml (3 tbsp) walnut oil in place of the butter.

TECHNIQUE

Stir the grated cheese into the creamy artichoke sauce and cook gently for 1 minute.

PENNE WITH OLIVES, ANCHOVY AND CHILLI

If you are lucky enough to find a local delicatessen with huge bowls of tasty olives marinating in flavoured oils, buy some to use in this recipe. They are usually far more delicious than olives found in jars or tins in super-markets and can be much cheaper. You probably won't need to add salt to this recipe as the ingredients themselves are naturally salty. Serve the pasta dish accompanied by a crisp leafy salad.

SERVES 4-6

400 g (14 oz) dried penne
2 garlic cloves
50 g (2 oz) can anchovies in olive oil
2.5 ml (½ tsp) dried chilli flakes
30 ml (2 tbsp) chopped fresh parsley
225 g (8 oz) stoned mixed black and green olives
60 ml (4 tbsp) extra-virgin olive oil
30-45 ml (2-3 tbsp) freshly grated Parmesan cheese
TO SERVE
extra Parmesan cheese

PREPARATION TIME
8-10 minutes
COOKING TIME
About 10 minutes
FREEZING
Not suitable

660-440 CALS PER SERVING

1. Bring a large saucepan of salted water to the boil. Add the pasta and cook until 'al dente', or according to packet instructions.

2. Meanwhile, peel and thinly slice the garlic cloves. Place in a saucepan with the anchovies and their oil. Add the chilli flakes and cook over a fairly high heat for 2-3 minutes, stirring to break up the anchovies with a wooden spoon; do not allow the garlic to brown. Stir in the parsley and remove from the heat.

3. Transfer the contents of the pan to a food processor and add the olives and olive oil. Process for a few seconds to give a coarse paste. Season with pepper to taste.

4. When the pasta is cooked, drain thoroughly in a colander. Return to the saucepan and add the pounded olive mixture and freshly grated Parmesan. Toss well to coat the pasta. Serve immediately, topped with Parmesan shavings.

VARIATION

Add some steamed broccoli or cauli-flower florets to the pasta and sauce with the grated Parmesan.

TECHNIQUE

Briefly process the olive, anchovy and garlic mixture to a coarse paste.

If you would like further information about the **Good Housekeeping Cookery Club**, please write to:
Penny Smith, Ebury Press, Random House, 20 Vauxhall Bridge Road, London SW1V 2SA.